Who Is God The Father?

Glimpses Of The Perfect Father

PART 2

OF

CAPTIVATED

BY THEIR

CHARACTER

ZOE Ministries International
P.O. Box 17036
Boulder, CO 80308-0036 USA
permissions@zoemin.org

All scripture quotations, unless otherwise indicated, are taken from the Holy Bible, New International Version ® NIV ® Copyright © 1973, 1978, 1984 by Biblica, Inc.®. Used by permission of Zondervan. All rights reserved worldwide. www.zondervan.com

Selected lessons are reprinted with permission from author Ruth Berry.

"Loving the Father" by Wes Daugenbaugh reprinted with permission from Christ for the Nations Institute.

"Journey to Adelphos" by Geoff Gorsuch is used by permission of Discipleship Journal. Copyright © (Issue 14, 1983), The Navigators. Used by permission of NavPress. All rights reserved. To subscribe, visit www.navpress.com or call (800) 877-1811.

Rev. 04/14

Dedication

It is with great love that we dedicate this course to Polly Wyant Thomas. Every day, this woman came before the throne of the Almighty King, praying for the staff, board and class members of ZOE Ministries International. Her vision for this ministry went beyond what the normal eye could see. Polly's tenacity before the throne was awe-inspiring. She was similar to Anna, the New Testament prophetess, who "never left the temple but worshiped night and day, fasting and praying."

We will greatly miss our precious Polly and her love for intercession on behalf of ZOE. However, we do know that she is now enjoying the beautiful presence of the Lord she knew so well here on earth. We thank You, Jesus, for giving us Polly!

Acknowledgments

ZOE Ministries International equips, trains and sends believers into the world to minister by the leading of the Holy Spirit. This dedicated ministry encourages God's people to use their gifts and talents in building the body of Christ for His glory. For that purpose, and with the Holy Spirit's leading, ZOE Ministries compiled this study guide. We wish to thank many faithful individuals for their support, time and talents, and to give our Lord all the praise and glory for this work!

WHO IS GOD THE FATHER?

LESSON 1

THE FATHER'S LOVE AND ACCEPTANCE..15

LESSON 2

RECONCILIATION 21

LESSON 3

ADOPTION..27

    "The Story of the Glove"
    ZOE Ministries International

LESSON 4

DEVELOPING OUR RELATIONSHIP WITH OUR FATHER......33

    "Loving the Father"
    Wes Daughenbaugh

LESSON 5

BUILDING SECURITY THROUGH DISCIPLINE................................45

    "His Plan for Me"
    Martha S. Nicholson

LESSON 6

AMBASSADORS..53

    "Journey to Adelphos"
    Geoff Gorsuch

For Further Study..69

Leader's Guide..75

About This Study

Who Is God the Father? is Part Two of a three-part study on the Trinity titled *Captivated by Their Character.*

Captivated by Their Character is designed to enrich your understanding of who God is—His character, His desires and plans. As you proceed through this Study Guide, you will examine what God says about Himself in the Bible. May God show you some glimpses of Himself as Father, Son and Holy Spirit.

Captivated by Their Character attempts to do the impossible! It tries to explain an invisible, dynamic God, who has revealed Himself to us humans as three persons. Although our finite minds may never fully plumb the depths of the mystery of God's full identity, we can gather some clues. The three different series in this study correspond to the three members of the Trinity. We suggest that you proceed through them in the arranged order—*Who Is Jesus, Who Is God the Father, Who Is the Holy Spirit.* Each series contains six lessons.

Each lesson in *Who Is God the Father* begins with an introduction or story. Specific Bible verses and corresponding questions follow. A related article is included with many lessons. May you come to know His complete goodness and passionate love for you.

For Self-Study

All that is required for this study is a Bible and an inquiring heart. After you read the questions posed in each lesson, record your response to the questions in the space provided or in a separate journal. We trust that as you meditate on the verses, God will, over time, draw you into an even closer relationship with Him.

For Use in a Small Group

For guidance in using this study in a small group setting, see the Leader's Guide section found in the back of this book.

Foreword

Has the subject of the Trinity ever brought confusion and frustration? The Father, Son and Holy Spirit are uniquely the same, and yet they have different roles. During this part of the study you will have the opportunity to examine what the Bible says about one person of the Trinity—God the Father.

Out of God's great love for the world, He sent His one and only Son as a living sacrifice in order to bring mankind back into relationship with Himself. Jesus, out of love and obedience to His Father, came to earth to fulfill God's plan and offered Himself as the once and for all sacrifice.

Before Jesus' death, He told His disciples that He would send the Holy Spirit to live in them and be with them forever. After Jesus' resurrection, the Father sent the Holy Spirit to live in all people who believe in Jesus as Lord. We would be totally "lost" without the Holy Spirit's presence in our lives.

The Trinity, three in one, may be a mystery; however, upon studying each person in the Trinity, we firmly believe that you will be *captivated by their character.* Our prayer is that God, by His Holy Spirit, will teach you all things, for His glory!

Dick and Ginny Chanda
Founding Directors
ZOE Ministries International

"Now this is eternal life [*zoe*]: that they may
know you, the only true God, and Jesus Christ,
whom you have sent."   *John 17:3*

"No one who denies the Son has the Father;
whoever acknowledges the Son has the Father
also."   *1 John 2:23*

"Jesus said, 'Anyone who has seen me has seen
the Father.' "   *John 14:9*

WHO IS GOD THE FATHER?   The Lord is gracious. He is
compassionate! He is slow to anger!   He is rich in love! (**Psalm
145:8**) This course introduces you to God the Father, who comes
to life and displays His love and generosity! Come get acquainted
with God as Father and see how He relates to us, His children.

For Self-Study
- It is strongly recommended that you complete the *Who Is
Jesus?* course before beginning this course.

- You will need a Bible for this course. As you proceed through
each lesson, prayerfully read the scriptures listed and record
your response to the questions in the space provided.

13

For Use in a Small Group

- It is assumed that you have completed the *Who Is Jesus?* course, as it is a prerequisite to this course and the *Who Is the Holy Spirit?* course.

- Please refer to the "Leader's Guide" section at the back of this book for guidance in leading/facilitating this course.

- Lessons 1–3 are designed to last one hour. You might want to allow 1 1/2 hours for Lessons 4–6, which contain more material.

- The course is designed to last six weeks. You may extend the course, as needed.

- Each participant will need a copy of this Study Guide, or you may copy the pages containing the questions, to give to participants.

- It is helpful to hand out copies of the same version of the Bible. Then participants can turn to a specific page number, making it easy for them to find a passage.

THE FATHER'S LOVE AND ACCEPTANCE

The Story of Kim-Binh (pronounced bin)
After the group Friends of Children of Vietnam was formed, the head of the group, a housewife, went to Vietnam to check on the progress of the orphanage. As she sat discussing the situation there with the woman who headed the orphans' care, she felt a pressure under her arm. Looking down, she discovered a beautiful Black-Vietnamese child snuggling close to her. The child was four year old Kim-Binh, an American GI baby who lived in the orphanage. Kim-Binh smiled at the lady and said, "I want to go with you and have you be my mother."

The lady set her mind to adopt the child right then, and before she left for America she had begun the adoption process. It was several months before Kim-Binh could actually walk through the door of her new home. During those months her future parents thought of her and sent her things she needed. They eagerly awaited the completion of the adoption, her trip to America, and her entry into the new family waiting for her.

Just as the lady knew about and prepared for Kim-Binh's arrival into her family, so God the Father knows us and prepares for each of us to come into His family.

Read **Psalm 139:1–18** silently or aloud.

1. How well acquainted is God with us?   What does He know about each of us?

2. Does God the Father love us as we are?

3. How was God's love demonstrated toward us?

   > **"You see, at just the right time, when we were still powerless, Christ died for the ungodly. Very rarely will anyone die for a righteous man, though for a good man someone might possibly dare to die. But God demonstrates His own love for us in this: While we were still sinners, Christ died for us."**   *Romans 5:6–8*

4. According to the following passage, who are those God has chosen?

   > **"...If God is for us, who can be against us? He who did not spare his own Son, but gave him up for us all—how will he not also, along with him, graciously give us all things? Who will bring any charge against those whom God**

has chosen? It is God who justifies. Who is he who condemns? Christ Jesus, who died—more than that, who was raised to life—is at the right hand of God and is also interceding for us. Who shall separate us from the love of Christ? Shall trouble or hardship or persecution or famine or nakedness or danger or sword? ...For I am convinced that neither death nor life, neither angels nor demons, neither the present nor the future, nor any powers, neither height nor depth, nor anything else in all creation, will be able to separate us from the love of God that is in Christ Jesus our Lord."

Romans 8:31–35, 38–39

God has chosen those who believe that Jesus is His Son and accept Jesus as their Savior.

5. Is there anything that you have thought separated you from God's love?

6. The Father's acceptance of us into His family is not based on

our good works or lifestyle, but on the completed work of Jesus
Christ and our response to that work.

> **"Praise be to the God and Father of our Lord
> Jesus Christ, who has blessed us in the heavenly
> realms with every spiritual blessing in Christ.
> For He chose us in Him before the creation of
> the world to be holy and blameless in His sight.
> In love He predestined us to be adopted as His
> sons through Jesus Christ, in accordance with
> His pleasure and will... ."**   *Ephesians 1:3–5*

According to the verse above, when did God choose us? Why
did He choose us?

_____

_____

_____

_____

7.   Sometimes it is hard to accept ourselves as we are. God the
     Father's love and acceptance of us should help us to accept
     ourselves. Even though we see our weaknesses, we know that
     He is in the process of transforming us to be like Jesus.

> **"And we know that in all things God works for
> the good of those who love Him, who have been
> called according to His purpose. For those God
> foreknew He also predestined *to be conformed
> to the likeness of His Son,* that He might be the
> firstborn among many brothers. And those He
> predestined, He also called; those He called,
> He also justified; those He justified, He also
> glorified.**

> **"What then shall we say in response to this?
> If God is for us, who can be against us? He
> who did not spare his own Son, but gave him**

up for us all—how will he not also, along with him [Jesus], graciously give us all things?"
                                        Romans 8:28–32

According to the passage above, what promises does God make to us, His children?

_____

_____

_____

_____

How incredibly gracious our Heavenly Father is! He knows us thoroughly, loves us anyway and has glorious plans for each of us, His children!

RECONCILIATION

Imagine yourself a citizen of a country in turmoil, desperately wanting to move to another, more peaceful country. You want to join family already there, but you are unable to meet the requirements for obtaining a visa. You have decided to sneak into this new country under cover of night. You have heard that it is hard to evade the border guards and that some people have been killed while trying to cross the border. Once you make it into the new country, you half-expect to get thrown out for not entering legally. If only you could obtain permission to cross the boundary that separates you from your relatives. If only you had a visa.

1. If you were such a citizen, what feelings would you have right now?

_____

_____

God the Father is holy and will not have fellowship with sin. We are unable to meet God's requirements for perfect holiness, so we are separated from God by our sin. However, the Father has provided a way into a love relationship with Him. Jesus is our visa.

> **"...Remember that at that time you were separate from Christ, excluded from citizenship in Israel and foreigners to the covenants of the promise, without hope and without God in the world. But now in Christ Jesus you who once were far away have been brought near through the blood of Christ ...Consequently, you are no longer foreigners and aliens, but fellow citizens with God's people and members of God's household... ."**   *Ephesians 2:12–13, 19*

Long before Jesus was born, God had given His chosen people, the Israelites, a way to obtain forgiveness of sin through animal sacrifice. But the blood sacrifice of these animals was only effective for sins already committed and they needed to sacrifice again and again. In addition, it did not deal with the root problem—our condition of unrighteousness before God.

2. According to the next two passages, what made it possible to be reconciled to God?

"For God was pleased to have all his fullness dwell in him [Jesus], and through him to reconcile to himself all things, whether things on earth or things in heaven, by making peace through his blood shed on the cross.

"Once you were alienated from God and were enemies in your minds because of your evil behavior. But now he has reconciled you by Christ's physical body through death to present you holy in his sight, without blemish and free from accusation... ."

Colossians 1:19–22

"All this is from God, who reconciled us to himself through Christ and gave us the ministry of reconciliation: that God was reconciling the world to himself in Christ, not counting men's sins against them. And he has committed to us the message of reconciliation...God made him who had no sin to be sin for us, so that in him we might become the righteousness of God."   *2 Corinthians 5:18–19, 21*

3. According to the following passage, what were we to God before we accepted Christ?

_____

_____

_____

"Since we have now been justified by his blood, how much more shall we be saved from his wrath through him! For if, when we were God's enemies, we were reconciled to him through the death of his Son, how much more, having been reconciled, shall we be saved through his life!"

Romans 5:9–10

4. And what are we to God once we accept Jesus as our Lord and Savior?

_____

_____

_____

Reconciliation or restoration of any broken relationship brings peace and healing to our lives.

Read the story of "The Prodigal Son."

> "A man had two sons. When the younger told his father, 'I want my share of your estate now, instead of waiting until you die!, his father agreed to divide his wealth between his sons.
>
> "A few days later this younger son packed all his belongings and took a trip to a distant land, and there wasted all his money on parties and prostitutes. About the time his money was gone a great famine swept over the land, and he began to starve. He persuaded a local farmer to hire him to feed his pigs. The boy became so hungry that even the pods he was feeding the swine looked good to him. And no one gave him anything.
>
> "When he finally came to his senses, he said to himself, 'At home even the hired men have food enough and to spare, and here I am, dying of hunger! I will go home to my father and say, "Father, I have sinned against both heaven and

you, and am no longer worthy of being called your son. Please take me on as a hired man." '

"So he returned home to his father. And while he was still a long distance away, his father saw him coming, and was filled with loving pity and ran and embraced him and kissed him.

"His son said to him, 'Father, I have sinned against heaven and you, and am not worthy of being called your son.'

"But his father said to the slaves, 'Quick! Bring the finest robe in the house and put it on him. And a jeweled ring for his finger and shoes! And kill the calf we have in the fattening pen. We must celebrate with a feast, for this son of mine was dead and has returned to life. He was lost and is found.' So the party began."

Luke 15:11–24 (The Living Bible)

5. What was the attitude of the prodigal son at the beginning of the story?

6. How do you think the father felt when his son demanded his share of his father's estate?

7. Yet what was the father's response to his son returning?

8. In this story the father represents God the Father and the son
    could be any one of us. How does God the Father feel about
    us when we sin and offend Him?

9. Is He willing to take us back when we come to Him?

ADOPTION

The Story of Vinh (pronounced Vin)

Vinh was nine years old when he was adopted by an American family. Vinh had been on his own since age three when his Vietnamese mother was killed. After her death, he survived totally by his own wits. He ate out of garbage heaps and learned to skillfully steal anything he needed or wanted without being caught. Vinh was brought to the orphanage by the Vietnamese authorities and ran away repeatedly, until he was adopted.

On Vinh's first day in his new home he greeted his new father's arrival home from work by taking him to the basement to show with pride what he had done for his new family. In the basement was every toy, every lawn chair, every mower, every movable object in the neighborhood, which Vinh had stolen without being seen. These he presented to his new father whom Vinh wanted very much to please.

1. If you were Vinh's new adoptive father, how would you handle
    this situation?

    _____

    _____

    _____

2. Read the following verses to see that we, like Vinh, have been
    adopted.

    > "But when the time had fully come, God sent
    > his Son, born of a woman, born under law,
    > to redeem those under the law, that we might
    > receive the full rights of sons. Because you are
    > sons, God sent the Spirit of his Son into our
    > hearts, the Spirit who calls out, 'Abba, Father.'
    > So you are no longer a slave, but a son; and since
    > you are a son, God has made you also an heir."
    >
    > *Galatians 4:4–7*

    > "Yet to all who received him, to those who
    > believed in his name, He gave the right to
    > become children of God—children born not
    > of natural descent, nor of human decision or a
    > husband's will, but born of God."
    >
    > *John 1:12–13*

    How do we qualify for adoption by God the Father?

    _____

    _____

    _____

Vinh's adoption was not based on his being the "perfect"
child, but on the love of his new parents. In the same way, we
are adopted by God not based on our merits, but based on His
love for us. He demonstrated His love toward us by sending
His only Son to earth and asking Him to die in our place. God

did this even though we are imperfect and in many ways like Vinh, trying to please our Father by what we think is right.

3. What benefits of adoption by God can you find in each of the following verses?

Re-read Galatians 4:4-7 from previous page.

"Praise be to the God and Father of our Lord Jesus Christ, who has blessed us in the heavenly realms with every spiritual blessing in Christ. For he chose us in him before the creation of the world to be holy and blameless in his sight. In love he predestined us to be adopted as His sons through Jesus Christ, in accordance with his pleasure and will—to the praise of his glorious grace, which he has freely given us in the One he loves. In him we have redemption through his blood, the forgiveness of sins, in accordance with the riches of God's grace that he lavished on us with all wisdom and understanding."
Ephesians 1:3–8

"...Because those who are led by the Spirit of God are sons of God. For you did not receive a spirit that makes you a slave again to fear, but you received the Spirit of sonship. And by him we cry, 'Abba, Father.' The Spirit himself testifies with our spirit that we are God's children. Now if we are children, then we are heirs—heirs of God and co-heirs with Christ, if indeed

> we share in his sufferings in order that we may
> also share in his glory."   *Romans 8:14–17*

4. What are the responsibilities we have as adopted children of
    God?

    _____

    _____

    _____

    _____

Vinh's adoptive father had to help Vinh unlearn some unacceptable behaviors, like stealing. We also, as God's children, need to come under His direction. God directs us as we read the Bible and listen to the Holy Spirit in us. In these ways we learn how to please our Heavenly Father. Vinh had to learn that his new father would provide all he needed. We need to realize that we don't have to provide for our needs by ungodly methods, but that God will provide what we need. When we are adopted by God the Father, we inherit all that is his.

5. What does God have that is now ours as His adopted children?

    _____

    _____

    _____

6. The Bible tells us to bring all our concerns to God in prayer.
    Prayer is simply talking to God.

    > "Do not be anxious about anything, but in
    > everything, by prayer and petition, with thanks-
    > giving, present your requests to God. And the
    > peace of God, which transcends all understand-
    > ing, will guard your hearts and your minds in
    > Christ Jesus."   *Philippians 4:6–7*

As an adopted child of God, is there something for which you would like to ask your heavenly Father? Or something for which you would like to thank Him?

_____

_____

_____

_____

Read **"The Story of the Glove."**

THE STORY OF THE GLOVE

As told by Ruth Berry*

Several years ago a woman went home to her father's funeral. She was assigned the task of taking care of his clothing. She cleaned out clothing from the closets, the drawers and the basement work area. Beside her father's bench were his work boots. They were leather, and completely formed to the shape of her father's feet. She had seen his boots all her life, different pairs, and the shape was always the same—definitely his. She could have picked his boots out from among one thousand boots. The Lord showed this woman a comparison between her father's boots and what God does in His children.

If you bought a pair of soft, leather gloves and went home and laid them on a table, they would have no character or ownership on them. But if you put them on the next morning and worked all day in them, that night when you laid them on the table, they would have changed shape just slightly. The gloves wouldn't be identifiable as yours, but they wouldn't be like they were the day you bought them. If you continued to wear them daily while you worked, each night you would notice more and more that the impression of your hands would be on the gloves. There would come a point where the gloves might even be uncomfortable for someone else to wear.

This is similar to what God does in us. When we are first born again, we appear no different than any other person. But as the Lord uses us in different situations, we begin to take on His look. Finally the time comes, either sooner or later, when we are identified with God because we "look" like Him. (Conversely, those who are used by Satan begin to resemble him.)

Sometimes people who come around us may mistakenly give us the credit for what the Lord is actually doing. An adoptive child may be told that he looks like his adoptive parent when, in fact, they are not genetically related. Similarly, we begin to take on some of God's characteristics after we've spent much time with Him.

> ** Ruth Berry is a former ZOE Staff member, who originally compiled most of this Who Is God the Father? curriculum. Ruth is remembered as a powerful woman of God who could meet and minister to virtually anyone. She and her husband, Norm, are now with the Lord.*

DEVELOPING OUR RELATIONSHIP
WITH OUR FATHER

1. How would you describe the "perfect father"?

_____

_____

_____

2. Describe what you think might be the "perfect child" for that father.

_____

_____

_____

3. Read the following scriptures to see how God the Father compares to our picture of the "perfect father."

> "Yet the Lord longs to be gracious to you; he rises to show you compassion. For the Lord is a God of justice. Blessed are all who

wait for him! O people of Zion, who live in Jerusalem, you will weep no more. How gracious he will be when you cry for help! As soon as he hears, he will answer you ...Whether you turn to the right or to the left, your ears will hear a voice behind you, saying, 'This is the way; walk in it.' "   *Isaiah 30:18–19, 21*

"Ask and it will be given to you; seek and you will find; knock and the door will be opened to you. For everyone who asks receives; he who seeks finds; and to him who knocks, the door will be opened.

"Which of you, if his son asks for bread, will give him a stone? Or if he asks for a fish, will give him a snake? If you, then, though you are evil, know how to give good gifts to your children, how much more will your Father in heaven give good gifts to those who ask him!"
     Matthew 7:7–11

"Ah, Sovereign Lord, you have made the heavens and the earth by your great power and outstretched arm. Nothing is too hard for you. You show love to thousands but bring the punishment for the fathers' sins into the laps of their children after them. O great and powerful God, whose name is the Lord Almighty, great are your purposes and mighty are your deeds. Your eyes are open to all the ways of men; you reward everyone according to his conduct and as his deeds deserve. You performed miraculous signs and wonders in Egypt and have continued them to this day, both in Israel and among all

> **mankind, and have gained the renown that is still yours."** *Jeremiah 32:17–20*

What are God's characteristics as mentioned in each passage?

_____

_____

_____

4. **Psalm 143** reveals one man's relationship with God. The author, David, was a shepherd. He belonged to the nation of Israel, God's chosen people, to whom God first revealed Himself. Read **Psalm 143**.

   What do you think David's relationship with God was like? Why?

   _____

   _____

   _____

5. A father-child relationship like David's does not happen accidentally. It requires time spent together and communication of affection, guidance, teaching and sometimes even discipline.

   What are ways we can get to know God the Father?

   _____

   _____

   _____

The following quote from A.W. Tozer's book, *The Pursuit of God*, mentions one way of getting to know God, i.e. reading the Bible.

> "For it is not mere words that nourish the soul, but God Himself, and unless and until the hearers find God in personal experience, they are not

the better for having heard the truth. The Bible is not an end in itself, but a means to bring men to an intimate and satisfying knowledge of God, that they may enter into Him, that they may delight in His Presence, may taste and know the inner sweetness of the very God Himself in the core and center of their hearts."[1]

As we spend time reading the Bible, certain verses will stand out in a way that lets us know God is speaking those words to us personally.

If you want to know what God the Father is like, read about Jesus. He is God made flesh, so that we can know God the Father better. **"Jesus answered, 'Anyone who has seen me has seen the Father' " John 14:9.**

We who have accepted Jesus Christ have been adopted into God's family. The dictionary defines adopt as "to take into one's family through legal means and raise as one's own child.[2]

6. According to the scripture below, upon what is our adoption and relationship with our Father God based?

    _____

    _____

    _____

    _____

> **"Then they asked him, 'What must we do to do the works God requires?' Jesus answered, 'The work of God is this: to believe in the one he sent.' "** *John 6:28–29*

7. According to the following passage, what are other ways we can communicate with God?

> " 'For I know the plans I have for you,' declares the Lord, 'plans to prosper you and not to harm you, plans to give you hope and a future. Then you will call upon me and come and pray to me, and I will listen to you. You will seek me and find me when you seek me with all your heart. I will be found by you,' declares the Lord... ."
>
> *Jeremiah 29:11–14a*

8. What different forms can prayer take?

9. How does God show His love for us?

> If needed, re-read **Isaiah 30:18–19, 21** and **Matthew 7:7–11** (from this lesson), and **Romans 8:28–32** (from Lesson 1) for hints.

10. According to the verses below, how do we show our love for God?

"This is love for God: to obey His commands." **1 John 5:3**

"And we pray this in order that you may live a life worthy of the Lord and may please him in every way: bearing fruit in every good work, growing in the knowledge of God... ."

Colossians 1:10

The Lord wants us to continually grow in our knowledge of and relationship with Him. As we grow in our understanding of Him, we allow God to change us and cause us to become who He created us to be.

"As the deer pants for streams of water, so my soul pants for you, O God."   Psalm 42:1

Just as the deer needs water to survive, so our spirits need God in order to be nourished and survive.

We show our love for God by admitting our need for Him and by trusting Him. It is part of God's plan for us to become more and more dependent on Him. This is the exact opposite of an earthly father's goal, which is to raise children able to function fully without him. This is because our fathers will not always be available. One big difference between God and our earthly fathers is that God will always be available to comfort us and give us wise counsel.

11. How can you improve your relationship with God? What steps are you willing to take this week to get to know your Father better?

12. In **John 14:6** Jesus said, **"No one comes to the Father except through me."** If you have never committed your life to Christ and you would like to, may we encourage you to pray the following prayer aloud? In this way, you can come to the Father through Jesus.

> **Dear Jesus,**
>
> **I know I have not always obeyed God's commands. I repent of my past behavior and ask you to please forgive me, and help me turn from everything that is displeasing to you.**
>
> **Thank you for showing me what the Father is like. Thank you for dying on the cross for me so that I could be forgiven and have a close relationship with the Father. Thank you for offering me forgiveness and the gift of your Spirit. I now receive those gifts by faith.**
>
> **Please come into my life by your Holy Spirit to be with me forever. Help me obey you and get to know you better. Be my leader, forgiver and friend, Amen.**

Read "Loving the Father."

LOVING THE FATHER

By Wes Daughenbaugh

I don't think it's possible to really love God with all your heart, soul, mind and strength until you know He loves you.

You'll never even get in the race until you have a revelation of God's love. That has to be the foundation of your life—your ministry. If that doesn't get through to you, you'll always be sort of limping along, but if you have this idea, "Jesus loves me," then who cares? Who cares about all the people who criticize you? Jesus loves you. You have a message to tell the world, not about yourself or who you are, but about Somebody who has your very being engraved on the palms of His hands—Somebody who loves you. When you know that, you have something to say!

"The Lord God, merciful and gracious, long-suffering, and abundant in goodness and truth, keeping mercy for thousands, forgiving iniquity and transgression and sin... ." *(Exod. 34:6,7)*

Where does love begin? "We love him, because he first loved us" (I John 4:19). Jesus prayed, "I in them, and thou in me, that they may be made perfect in one; and that the world may know that thou hast sent me, and hast loved them, as thou hast loved me" (John 17:23). Jesus is saying that God loves you as much as He loves His Son. He could have sent us all to hell to satisfy His justice, but He wouldn't have satisfied His *love!* So He sentenced us to death, and then He came down and died for us and satisfied both!

Jesus has made a way for all of us to become acceptable. A lot of people are all messed up, because they haven't had enough love when they were children. God has two kinds of love: *acceptance* and *approval.* Acceptance is what you do with a bunch of little kids. You get them on your lap and hug them, pat them on the head, tickle them. Someone might ask, "'What did those kids do for you to love them so much?'" Nothing. They are just kids; that's all they need to be! What have you done that God should love you? You're His kids. He made you in His image, for His pleasure. His pleasure wasn't to create you so you could bring in the evening paper like a dog. Some people think they're created for God's pleasure so He can just boss them around and make errand-boys out of them.

God started speaking to me about how to love Him. He didn't tell me a bunch of ways to love Him. He gave me the names of several people and told me to love Him as they did:

1) *Love Me like Mary who sat at My feet.* Luke 10:39-42 tells the story about Mary who sat at the Lord's feet listening, and Martha who was much distracted by the preparations that had to be made. Jesus told Martha that Mary had chosen the better thing which would not be taken away from her. Mary had an appetite for the Word of God. As you learn to love the Word of God, you learn to love Jesus. You're never far away from sin, and you must have an appetite for the love letters of Jesus and get excited about His work. That's the spirit you must have when you're reading the Word, that the Word is always a treat, never drudgery. You have to decide to be like Mary about the Word, because a lukewarm attitude about God's Word is a lukewarm attitude toward God.

2) *Love Me like John who leaned on My breast.* At the Last Supper, Jesus had just said that one was going to betray Him; and everyone was looking around wondering who it was. Simon Peter whispered to John to "Ask Him who it is." So, John, with his head on Jesus' breast, asked, "Lord, who is it?" I didn't know what that meant. I asked, "Lord, how do I do that? How do I lean on Jesus' breast?" Then I understood: John heard the heartbeat of Jesus as he leaned on Jesus' breast. I believe we have to be close enough to God in prayer that we begin to feel what He feels, to feel His heartbeat. It beats for individuals. It cares for people. You have to get alone with God and spend time in prayer. It's not how many tapes you listen to, how many books you read nor how many TV shows you watch; what counts is, "Are you hearing His heartbeat?" That only comes from time spent in prayer.

3) *Love Me like the Good Samaritan.* The Good Samaritan helped somebody who was hurting. Jesus said there would come a day when he could say, "Come, ye blessed of my Father; inherit the kingdom prepared for you...For I was hungry and ye gave me food..." (Matt. 25:34-35). When you love Jesus like the Good Samaritan loved Him, you're going to have a great love for hurting people. He's touched by our infirmities. He feels what we feel. When we hurt, He hurts. If you hurt today, I guarantee it – Jesus hurts! If somebody can alleviate your hurt, then Jesus says, "Oh that brings relief to Me."

4) *Love Me like the woman who washed My feet.* There were two separate occasions where someone washed Jesus' feet and anointed them. One was at a Pharisee's house (Luke 7:37-38). The woman was a sinner but she was watching Jesus, this good man who had set her free from demons, from her life of sin, and the Pharisees weren't treating Him right. They hadn't even given Him the common courtesy to wash His feet. Jesus had first loved her; so, she brought some perfume in an alabaster box; and she sat down at His feet and started weeping out her love for Him and for His neglected feet. Having no towel, she dried His feet with her hair. When she was done, she poured perfume all over them.

The other woman was Mary. It happened in Bethany at Simon the leper's house. Lazarus was sitting at the table; Martha was serving; and Mary came in with a pound of spikenard, poured it over Jesus' head; and the house was filled with its fragrance. Mark 14 tells the same story. Everybody has an alabaster jar. It's the best part of your life that you're saving for yourself. Mary was saving that ointment for her burial. The people saved this expensive stuff, so when they died it could be poured over their stinking flesh. You might as well break it. Human pride has to be broken. There's an alabaster jar of our ego where we want the glory and want to be somebody. God may call you to serve Him in a place where your name is never in lights and nobody knows you're serving Him with all your blood, sweat and tears. But when you break that box, you're not pouring it on men for their praise; it's for Jesus. Pouring it on His head means to give Him all the praise and honor, but pouring it on His feet means you're honoring His ministers. The feet of the body are the ministers. They carry the weight of responsibility, and they take the most abuse. Just like the feet carrying the weight of the body, kicking into the sand, getting hot, tired and sweaty, ministers all over the world, God's chosen servants are bearing the heat of the day for Him. They are hurting, and don't you be someone who wants to criticize.

5) Love Me like Abraham who obeyed Me. God spoke to Abraham to leave his land, family, and relatives for a strange land. Abraham took off! It's not always easy to leave your family behind. But if you have a call to the mission field, you may have to do just that. It's not always easy to obey God. But when you obey Him, you really love Him. He said, "He that hath my command-ments, and keepeth them, he it is that loveth me" (John 14:21). That involves sexual purity, watching your spiritual intake and all those spiritual commands. When you read the Bible, don't just look for promises; look for new verses you can obey. That's how we love Jesus—by obeying Him like Abraham did.

It's not your reputation, talents, how smart you are, how pretty or handsome that counts. What really counts is: Do you love Jesus? Do you love God? The Bible says that in the end times the love of many will grow cold, because iniquity will abound. We're in those days right now, and there aren't too many people who keep loving Jesus fervently and don't cool off. Say, "Lord, I want to do something more for You. I thirst to bring You glory. I just want to love You more. How can I love You more?" Remember, He first loved you!

Excerpt from a message given at Christ For The Nations Institute. Wes Daughenbaugh is a teacher/evangelist who trav-els nationally and internationally holding revival seminars.

Reprinted with permission from CFNI.

BUILDING SECURITY THROUGH DISCIPLINE

More of the Story of Vinh (pronounced Vin)

As we read before, Vinh was nine years old when he was adopted by an American family. Vinh had been on his own since age three when his Vietnamese mother was killed. After her death, he survived totally by his own wits. He ate out of garbage heaps and learned to skillfully steal anything he needed or wanted without being caught. He was brought to the orphanage by the Vietnamese authorities and ran away repeatedly, until he was adopted.

On Vinh's first day in his new home he greeted his father's arrival home from work by taking him to the basement to show, with pride, what he had done for his new family. In the basement was every toy, every lawn chair, every mower, every movable object in the neighborhood that Vinh had stolen without being seen. These he presented as a gift to his new father, whom Vihn wanted very much to please.

Vinh also went shopping at the grocery store with his parents. After leaving the store he opened his coat to reveal many products he had stolen from the store, invisibly to his parents, which had to be returned. The next time they went shopping, his parents insisted that he keep his hands on the cart handle at all times. Even then he still was able to attach things to the inside of his coat.

One day at school Vinh was talking to his teacher across the desk, on top of which was a small box of coins used to teach the class how to make change. At the end of the conversation the teacher found that Vinh had pocketed the coins from the box without her seeing it.

1. What amount of patience do you imagine Vihn's parents had to have as they disciplined and trained Vinh not to steal?

_____

_____

_____

God the Father is even more patient with us as He disciplines us. *Discipline* can be defined as "to train by instruction and control."[1] Antonyms of the word *discipline* are chaos, disorder, rebellion and mutiny. Synonyms include order, government, regulation, training and instruction.

We become a disciple, a follower or student of Jesus, as we yield to His discipline.

2. According to the following verse, what does it show when God disciplines us?

> **"My son, do not despise the Lord's discipline and do not resent His rebuke, because the Lord disciplines those He loves, as a Father the son he delights in."**   *Proverbs 3:11–12*

_____

_____

_____

3. Read **Hebrews 12:5–11**. This passage says that discipline can

be harsh or unpleasant. Is God ever too hard or harsh with us?

What does the following verse reveal about God the Father?

> "Fathers, do not irritate and provoke your children to anger [do not exasperate them to resentment] but rear them [tenderly] in the training and discipline and the counsel and admonition of the Lord." *Ephesians 6:4*
> (The Amplified Bible)

The Lord tells parents to be tender and caring with their children the way He is with us.

4. According to the verse below, how does God the Father discipline us?

> "All scripture is God-breathed and is useful for teaching, rebuking, correcting and training in righteousness, so that the man of God may be thoroughly equipped for every good work." *2 Timothy 3:16*

God uses His Word, the Bible, to instruct and correct us.

In the next passage the Word is compared to a mirror. We

look into the Word and it reveals the dirt and grime in our lives, which needs to be cleansed. As we apply the truth of the Word in our lives, a cleansing occurs.

> **"Do not merely listen to the word, and so deceive yourselves. Do what it says. Anyone who listens to the word but does not do what it says is like a man who looks at his face in the mirror and, after looking at himself, goes away and immediately forgets what he looks like. But the man who looks intently into the perfect law that gives freedom, and continues to do this, not forgetting what he has heard, but doing it—he will be blessed in what he does."**
>
> ***James 1:22–25***

5. According to **James 1:22–25** (above), what is the result of doing God's Word?

   _____

   _____

   _____

When we are not obedient to what God says in the Word, God allows the natural consequences of our sin to affect us. Those natural consequences can be very effective in training us.

6. How else does God discipline us?

   _____

   _____

   _____

God can use circumstances to train us. There are times when life's circumstances seem too hard to endure. But God promises us in the Bible that He will show us the way out of temptation if we keep looking to Him!

> "No temptation has seized you except what
> is common to man. And God is faithful; he
> will not let you be tempted beyond what you
> can bear. But when you are tempted, he will
> also provide a way out so that you can stand up
> under it." *1 Corinthians 10:13*

The temptation here does not come from God.

> "When tempted, no one should say, 'God
> is tempting me.' For God [in you] cannot be
> tempted by evil, nor does he tempt anyone;
> but each one is tempted when, by his own evil
> desire, he is dragged away and enticed."
> *James 1:13–14*

God is not the source of temptations, but He can use them to
train us.

7. How could God turn a temptation into something that would
   benefit us or other people?

   _____

   _____

   _____

God's work in us is like the purification of gold. Gold has to
be heated to a very high temperature several times, and the
impurities skimmed off, before it becomes pure gold.

8. What is God the Father's ultimate purpose in disciplining us
   as stated in the following verses?

   > "...Christ loved the church and gave himself
   > up for her to make her holy, cleansing her by
   > the washing with water through the word, and
   > to present her to himself as a radiant church,

without stain or wrinkle or any other blemish,
but holy and blameless." *Ephesians 5:25b–27*

"...It [discipline] produces a harvest of righteousness and peace for those who have been
trained by it."   *Hebrews 12:11*

"For our light and momentary troubles are
achieving for us an eternal glory that far out-
weighs them all."   *2 Corinthians 4:17*

"Here is a trustworthy saying: If we died with
him, we will also live with him; if we endure,
we will also reign with him. If we disown him,
he will also disown us; if we are faithless, he
will remain faithful, for he cannot disown himself."   *2 Timothy 2:11–13*

9. According to **2 Timothy 2:11–13** (above), what plans does
    God have for us?

The Father's discipline makes us fit to spend eternity with our
holy God and to reign in heaven with Christ. Also, as God
changes our lives, others will see it and be drawn to Jesus.
Discipline trains us so that God can send us out into the world
around us. (See Lesson 6.)

Our training by God is like that of a concert pianist. He
has long, difficult hours of practice that are unseen by the concert audience, but that produce the finished product of great
skill.

You only invest time and training into something of value.

The fact that God disciplines us or trains us proves that He loves us. We are worthy of His time and loving care.

Read **"His Plan for Me"** now.

10. Do you believe that God loves you enough to discipline you?

11. Why does discipline seem painful to us?

12. Can you think of an area in your life about which the Lord has been trying to get your attention? An area He desires to discipline?

HIS PLAN FOR ME

Martha Snell Nicholson

When I stand at the Judgment Seat of Christ
And He shows me His plan for me,
The plan of my life as it might have been,
Had He had His way; and I see

How I blocked Him here, and checked Him there,
And I would not yield my will,
Will there be grief in my Saviour's eyes,
Grief though He loves me still?

He would have me rich, but I stand here poor,
Stripped of all but His grace,
While memory runs like a hunted thing
Down the paths I cannot retrace.

Then my desolate heart will well nigh break
With the tears I cannot shed;
I shall cover my face with my empty hands;
And bow my uncrowned head.

Lord of the years that are left to me,
I give them to thy hand;
Take me and break me, mold me to
The pattern Thou hast planned.

LESSON 6

AMBASSADORS

During this course we have looked at our relationship with our Father God.

1. What is our relationship to God the Father?

2. According to the verse below, what is the Father's attitude toward the world?

> "For God so loved the world that he gave his one and only Son, that whoever believes in him shall not perish but have eternal life."
>
> **John 3:16**

He loves the world! Look at the cost of reconciliation to God!
He gave Jesus.

3. According to the following verses, what did Jesus do while He
    lived on earth?

> " 'My food,' said Jesus, 'is to do the will of him
> who sent me and to finish his work.' "
>
> *John 4:34*

> "For my Father's will is that everyone who
> looks to the Son and believes in him shall have
> eternal life, and I will raise him up at the last
> day."   *John 6:40*

> "For I did not speak of my own accord, but the
> Father who sent me commanded me what to say
> and how to say it. I know that his command
> leads to eternal life. So whatever I say is just
> what the Father has told me to say."
>
> *John 12:49–50*

Jesus acted as an ambassador to the earth from God the
Father. The dictionary defines ambassador as an "authorized
messenger or representative." [1]

4. What is the message that Jesus delivered?

5. What is the eternal life mentioned above in the verses from
    the book of **John**?

How does the following verse define eternal life?

> **"Now this is eternal life: that they may know you, the only true God, and Jesus Christ, whom you have sent."** *John 17:3*

6. How is Jesus' definition of eternal life different from ours?

Knowing God—knowing the Father and Jesus—is eternal life. Jesus' desire and purpose is to give us eternal life and to make the Father known! He wants to bring all people back into a relationship with God as their Father.

> **"I have revealed you [Father] to those whom you gave me out of the world. They were yours; you gave them to me and they have obeyed your word. Now they know everything you have given me comes from you. For I gave them the words you gave me and they accepted them. They knew with certainty that I came from you, and they believed that you sent me."** *John 17:6–8*

> **"Righteous Father, though the world does not know you, I know you, and they know that you have sent me. I have made you known to them,**

and will continue to make you known in order
that the love you have for me may be in them
and that I myself may be in them."

John 17:25–26

7. Do most people know of the Father's personal love for them?

_____

_____

_____

_____

Many won't know that God loves them unless we tell them.

"How, then, can they call on the one they have
not believed in? And how can they believe in
the one of whom they have not heard? And
how can they hear without someone preaching
to them? And how can they preach unless they
are sent?"   Romans 10:14–15

"As you sent me into the world, I have sent them
[Jesus' disciples] into the world...My prayer is
not for them alone. I pray also for those who
will believe in me through their message, that
all of them may be one, Father, just as you are
in me and I am in you. May they also be in us
so that the world may believe that you have sent
me."   John 17:18, 20–21

"We are therefore Christ's ambassadors, as
though God were making his appeal through
us. We implore you on Christ's behalf: Be reconciled to God."   2 Corinthians 5:20

We are called to be ambassadors of Christ, representing Him and bringing His message of a love relationship with God the Father.

Read *"Journey to Adelphos"* now.

8. What does the Lord ask us to do?

    _____

    _____

    _____

    _____

    a. Be Jesus' disciples.

        "To the Jews who had believed him, Jesus said, 'If you hold to my teaching, you are really my disciples.' "   *John 8:31*

        "A new command I give you: Love one another. As I have loved you, so you must love one another. By this all men will know that you are my disciples, if you love one another."
        John 13:34–35

    b. Take the Good News of the Gospel into the world. Tell them that God desires to save them from the penalty of their sins.

        "...Go into all the world and preach the good news to all creation. Whoever believes and is baptized will be saved, but whoever does not believe will be condemned."   *Mark 16:15–16*

        "He [Jesus] told them, 'This is what is written: The Christ will suffer and rise from the dead on the third day, and repentance and forgiveness of

sins will be preached in his name to all nations,
beginning at Jerusalem.' "   *Luke 24:46–47*

c. Make disciples.

"...All authority in heaven and on earth has
been given to me. Therefore go and make disciples of all nations, baptizing them in the name
of the Father and of the Son and of the Holy
Spirit, and teaching them to obey everything I
have commanded you. And surely I am with
you always, to the very end of the age."
                                    Matthew 28:18–20

However, we are not supposed to be Jesus' disciples and
share the Good News and make disciples with our own
strength. God the Father wants to empower us to be His
witnesses.

"You are witnesses of these things. I am going
to send you what my Father has promised; but
stay in the city until you have been clothed with
power from on high."   *Luke 24:48–49*

"But you will receive power when the Holy
Spirit comes on you; and you will be my wit-
nesses in Jerusalem, and in all Judea and
Samaria, and to the ends of the earth."
                                         Acts 1:8

The next course will be *Who Is the Holy Spirit?*

Adelphos is brotherhood, the place where brothers live.
There, at the end of a hard road, life is found,
and the shameful self forgotten.

JOURNEY TO ADELPHOS
One Man's Walk

By Geoff Gorsuch

I WAS WILLING to leave my fishing nets for the Revolution. My reasons were good enough—Roman oppression, the daily nonsense in the temple, our longing for Solomon's glory. My wife didn't fully understand, but she accepts it. I had to do it. He asked me to. "Follow me," he said.

Returning now to Jerusalem, he says this time will be the last. He has spoken of suffering and death, but he doesn't seem to understand how popular he really is. Look at them: "Hosanna!" They're welcoming their new king. They want to give him the crown. They love him!

Sometimes I just can't figure him out. I tried to explain all this to him, but he wouldn't hear it. He rebuked me.

But they love him!

Then again, look at them. Misfits. Can we restore the kingdom with these outcasts of law and tradition—the spurned of God? There must be something else.

Maybe that's why he's returning to Jerusalem. Once he gets his hands on the power....

I wonder: Is that what James and John were thinking the day they asked for it all? They have confidence in Jesus and his kingdom, but they too must realize that those who surround him are certainly not the hope of the future. To recreate Solomon's glory with prostitutes and lepers and others whose commitment is only skin deep seems too much to ask.

And after all, Matthew is only a tax collector. How can we trust him?

So James and John opted for position. Why shouldn't I? The nerve! In front of us all they asked for the key posts in his new kingdom. You should have heard the murmuring. We all have expectations and plans of our own.

The Lord's response was simple: "Can you drink the cup?" Now they realize that authority brings with it certain "responsibilities."

James says they can handle it. John says he feels he knows where Jesus is going and how he and James can best contribute. Of course they can drink the cup!

NOW WE KNOW THAT THE CUP HAD NOTHING to do with Solomon's glory—but with God's.

Jesus himself was able to drink it only after sweating great drops of blood in agonized prayer. He asked his Father three times if the cup could pass from him. But he received only silence.

In peace he uttered, "Not my will, but thine be done." Destiny's words.

In light of what followed, he was amazingly serene. "For this moment I have come," he told us.

Then the calm was shattered as the powers that be were led to him by torchlight and the traitor's kiss. Only hours before, I had promised to be faithful to the end. I drew the sword of illusory and easy courage, and struck the first blow of Revolution. Surely now they had forced his hand! Surely now he would act!

At the sight of blood, hands began to reach for weapons and fear flashed in the eyes of all—all except one. Love seized the initiative. His hand reached out and healed the wound I had just caused. My revolution was over. His began.

I couldn't believe it. In just a few minutes my illusions were shattered by the realities he calmly accepted. Certainly the angels awaited his beck and call. He could save himself. Why didn't he?

We were scandalized as the one greater than Solomon went to a criminal's trial whose foregone conclusion was obvious to all. The spectacle revealed not the guilt of the accused, but the depravity of the accusers.

Jesus would see it through, with or without us. He wanted us to follow not an age-old battle cry of revolution, but him. Yet we couldn't. We just couldn't.

Disillusion led to fear and fear to panic. We scattered. At a distance I watched as he remained silent.

Decadent Power demanded proof, then shrugged, "What is truth?"

Then, watching him hanging, Respectability taunted. "Save yourself. Come down from the cross, then we'll believe."

He didn't because he knew they wouldn't. The crown of thorns on his obedient brow crushed everyone's self-justifying illusion. Even our own loyalty, when put to the test, went out with the tide of popular opinion. When it finally came to choices—for fear of the crowd, for a few pieces of silver, for a few minutes of warmth by a fire—we abandoned him. Our final allegiance was to our own skins.

Truth stood alone. Its revolution will forever belong only to him. He had promised that it would succeed, but only in his way. The world now sees the price.

God died.

It was over. There was nothing left for us, and we began to wonder if there ever had been. Had we been fools? Judas, not finding forgiveness with the priests in the temple or with himself, cast his coveted silver aside and hung himself. I threw away the sword.

James and John no longer talk of their position in the kingdom, but of the value of the kingdom. The price of his obedience has demonstrated the worthiness of Christ. Have we realized it too late?

WE WERE BECALMED ON THE water. The nets were empty.

"Cast your nets on the other side!" came the call from shore.

John said it was *him*!

I needed assurance from him, perhaps more than the others. I had not only fled from him, but also verbally denied him. I was torn between joy and shame.

As I splashed desperately to shore, my reticence at seeing again the Lord whom I had denied melted as our eyes met. All was forgiven. But could I ever forgive myself? Wasn't it really too late? Not once, but *three times* I had renounced his name.

Later as we ate together Jesus asked me a simple question that cut like a knife: "Peter, do you love me?"

I had once been willing to die gloriously for him, but now I had no pretty speeches. Now I knew myself. I pondered the choice I had made. I painfully remembered.

He was relentless: "Do you love me? Do you love me?" Gently he probed to show me the depth of his love and to convince me it wasn't too late.

"O Lord, you know all things," I finally said.

Three times he returned, "Tend my lambs"—three affirmations that erased my three denials. He commissioned me as a shepherd, and rebuilt me as a man.

There was nothing to add. He had forgiven mankind, and I was to care for them. I was called not to the vainglorious attempt to win a victory, but to the work of caring for those for whom the victory already had been won. There was no greater victory than the cross, which days before had scattered us in shame. There was no other hero, no other glory.

Just obedience. We drank the cup.

Now the Holy Spirit can come. We have been well prepared. Our Lord ascended, and left us with one another and with a mission, a great commission: "Go!"

Our imperfections, so glaringly apparent when we were with him, are still there, but each of us has faced the cross—or should I say, the self that the cross revealed – and let our illusions die. In hoping to be served, we have been reduced to servants.

In our revealed weakness, we are finding each other's strengths. By following Him—even to the cross—we have found each other. To love "as I have loved" is his great commandment by which his great commission will be accomplished.

We have been reduced to love. We are brothers.
I embraced Matthew.
The Revolution was on.

Reprinted with permission from Discipleship Journal.

Who Is God the Father?

MAGAZINE LIST

For your convenience we have included the following list of magazines from which this course's articles have been drawn. If you wish to receive these magazines on a regular basis, the information below may help.

Christ For the Nations
P.O. Box 769000
(800) 933-CFNI
Dallas, TX 75376-9000
www.cfni.org

Discipleship Journal
Subscriber Services
(800) 829-3346
P.O. Box 5548
Harlan, IA 51593-1048
www.navpress.com/Magazines/DiscipleshipJournal/Contact

Father, Lesson 4

  1. A.W. Tozer, *The Pursuit of God* (Camp Hill, PA: Christian Publications, Inc., 1948), from the Preface.

  2. William Morris, Ed., *The American Heritage Dictionary of the English Language* (Boston, Massachusetts: American Heritage Publishing Co., Inc. and Houghton Mifflin Company, 1969), pp. 17–18.

Father, Lesson 5

  1. Ibid., p. 375.

Father, Lesson 6

  1. Ibid., p. 40.

To develop your relationship with God, we recommend the following courses offered by ZOE Ministries International.

For new believers, we recommend completing the Who Is Jesus?, Who Is God the Father?, Who Is the Holy Spirit? and Hearing God's Voice courses before taking other ZOE courses.

Who Is Jesus?
Jesus is the Word! Jesus is life! Jesus is light! This course introduces you to Jesus as the Word, who comes to life and shines forth light by which to live! Come get acquainted with Jesus and see how He relates to people as individuals.

Who Is God the Father?
The Lord is gracious. He is compassionate! He is slow to anger! He is rich in love! (Psalm 145:8) This course introduces you to God the Father, who comes to life and displays His love and generosity. Come get acquainted with God as Father and see how He relates to us, His children.

Who Is the Holy Spirit?
He is the Counselor, Comforter and Helper! He teaches and guides us! The Father sent Him to be with us permanently.
This course introduces you to the Holy Spirit, who comes to life and empowers us to become more like Jesus. Come get acquainted with the Holy Spirit and see how He relates to us as our Helper.

HEARING COURSES

Hearing God's Voice

In this course, everyone is encouraged to participate by applying the principles they read in scripture in order to learn to recognize when the Holy Spirit is speaking. The inner knowing, inner voice, and the authoritative voice of the Holy Spirit are discussed, as well as other manifestations of the Holy Spirit. The Lord is personal and unique, and desires to communicate with each one of His sheep in a personal and unique manner! (This course is a prerequisite for all the following courses except for *How to Hear God's Voice—In Marriage*.)

How to Hear God's Voice—In Christ

In the *Hearing God's Voice* course we learned how to hear God as individuals, whereas in the In Christ course, we learn how the body of Christ operates together under His direction and to His glory. We look at Romans 12 and examine the motive gifts that determine our individual bents. This study enables us to understand, appreciate and love each other. We also look at the Trinity and how they operate together. We learn about the precious person of the Holy Spirit and how He teaches, guides and comforts us. We also learn about the gifts of the Holy Spirit in 1 Corinthians 12 and 14 brought about as the Holy Spirit moves through us. Participants have remarked that this course has enabled them to see people the way God sees them and how they fit in the body of Christ.

How to Hear God's Voice—In Marriage

This course is based on the love relationship God had with mankind in the very beginning. We examine our attitudes toward each other and how they reflect the greatest love of all, the love of Christ. Do we love and honor each other with the unconditional love that our Lord Jesus had for us while dying on the cross? As in previous courses, we examine scripture, seek the Lord, and ask Him, "How can I better serve and love my spouse?" We discover how we complete each other, not compete with each other.

How to Hear God's Voice—In Family

In today's society we see the growing deterioration of the family. Parents are confused about what the Bible teaches on family issues. During this course we examine scriptures and what it means to: "Train up a child [early childhood] in the way he should go [and in keeping with his individual bent], and when he is old [teen years can be the best] he will not depart from it." (AMP with additions)

http://www.zoeministries.org/hearing-gods-voice/

KNOWING COURSES

How to Know God's Voice—In Intimate Friendship

Intimate Friendship with God! Can we experience such a relationship with the Creator of the universe? Here we examine what the Bible teaches us about the fear of the Lord, and how we can, indeed, have a deeper, more intimate relationship with Him. This is a very personal, yet freeing course on growing intimacy with God.

How to Know God's Voice—In Worship

The focus of this course is on ministering to the Lord. During our time together the Lord draws us corporately into His presence as we worship Him. We study what worship is, why we worship, and how we worship.

How to Know God's Voice—In His Presence
The Lord is calling each one of His sheep to come into His presence and to know Him in a deeper way. This course is not for
the new believer nor the faint in heart. Those who are serious
about knowing the Father in a more intimate way will find this
course challenging but rewarding. Examining Jesus' last days on
earth will direct us into the presence of the Lord. This course is
for those who have completed other ZOE courses.

How to Know God's Voice—In the Coming of the Lord
Many are proclaiming dates and times when the Lord Jesus will
return for His bride. This course is designed to focus on our prep-
aration for His coming, not when He is coming, and to better
understand the Lord's statement of Revelation 22:20: "Yes, I am
coming." It is the goal of this course to prepare ourselves as the
bride of Christ, with hearts that will respond with "Amen. Come,
Lord Jesus."

http://www.zoeministries.org/knowing-gods-voice/

FOLLOWING COURSES

How to Follow God's Voice—In Healing

During this course we examine the scriptures in which Jesus
healed the sick. The Holy Spirit highlights these passages as we
study, and our faith increases! We realize that Jesus is the Healer,
and we are simply His vessels as we listen to and follow His voice.

How to Follow God's Voice—In Power
Evangelism is often thought of as a bad word! In this course we
come to realize that God has a special plan for evangelism for us
if we are only sensitive and obedient to His voice. Preparing your

testimony, leading someone in salvation, and discipling others are a few of the topics discussed in this course. This is a real life-changer as we minister in "power evangelism!"

How to Follow God's Voice—In Intercession

Jesus is in constant intercession (Hebrews 7:25). As we come before Him in worship, intercession is a natural outflow of our relationship with Him. By yielding to the Holy Spirit, our ministry to others through intercession will increase.

How to Follow God's Voice—In Spiritual Warfare

As we come to know and recognize who our Lord is, He reveals to us who He is not! The tactics of Satan and our spiritual weapons are defined in this course. The Lord leads us in spiritual warfare as He enlists and mobilizes His army!

http://www.zoeministries.org/following-gods-voice/

ONE-ON-ONE DISCIPLESHIP

Discipleship by the Word of God and the Power of the Holy Spirit.

This 12-week course was developed by a disciple-maker after many years of successful one-on-one discipleship. Through this method the Holy Spirit is allowed to minister to the disciple through the Word and the encouragement of the disciple-maker. No other techniques or methods are used.

The entire course has been designed to enable individuals to feel confident in making disciples as directed by our Lord: *"Therefore go and make disciples of all nations …."* Matthew 28:19.

Not only do the participants learn what discipleship means according to the Word of God, but they are encouraged to participate in a one-on-one discipleship program as part of the course. This training allows individuals to take great strides in their personal relationship with God and in ministry. It changes lives in a very simple, yet powerful way.

http://www.zoeministries.org/one-on-one-discipleship/

For more information on courses offered by ZOE Ministries International, please visit the ZOE website at www.zoeministries.org.

LEADER´S GUIDE

Leader's Guide

Leading others into a deeper relationship with God is close to the Father's heart! May He enable you to communicate His love to the members of your group.

Time Frame

Even though each series is designed to last six weeks, you may extend the study as needed. For *Who Is Jesus?*, we suggest you allow about an hour for your group to proceed through the readings and to share their answers to the questions. The first three lessons of *Who Is God the Father?* should last about an hour as well. For the latter half of *Who Is God the Father?* and all of *Who Is the Holy Spirit?*, you will find it necessary to allow up to 1½ hours. More time may be needed for your meeting if reading the Bible is a new skill for participants.

Study Materials

The materials that participants need for this study include a Bible and a copy of this Study Guide. When a lesson has separate versions for the participant and the facilitator, you will lead the lesson from the facilitator's version.

If the members of your small group are not familiar with the Bible, you may want to distribute identical versions of the Bible. Then, as you find the assigned passage, you can refer them to a specific page number. By the time your group begins *Who Is the Holy Spirit?*, participants are expected to bring their own Bible.

The material covered in the three series, *Who Is Jesus?*, *Who Is God the Father?*, *Who Is the Holy Spirit?*, progressively becomes more complex. This is one reason why we recommend that you complete the series in the suggested order.

Class Format

Greet Group Members
Personally greet each person as they arrive. As facilitator, you want to create an atmosphere of joy, caring and acceptance. Remember that the joy of the Lord is your strength (Nehemiah 8:10). The more comfortable people are, the more they will participate in the discussions. Be sure the meeting location is conducive to discussion and learning.

Distribute Class Materials
Distribute Bibles at the beginning of each lesson. Participants should bring their Study Guide to each meeting. Provide pens or pencils for those who want to write answers in their Study Guide.

Open With Prayer
After study materials have been distributed, open the lesson with a short, simple prayer. You are serving as a model for praying aloud in a small group setting. In later lessons as the group becomes comfortable with the format and with each other, you might want to ask a participant ahead of time to open the lesson with a short prayer.

Lead the Discussion
Begin the discussion time by asking a participant to read aloud the opening paragraph(s). The more participants are given the chance to speak or read, the more likely they will share during the discussion.

Pose the questions from the facilitator's version of the lesson. When possible, ask participants to read the Bible verses. Allow people time to absorb the meaning of the scripture and to formulate an answer. You may want to repeat or rephrase the question.

Periods of silence are acceptable.

If someone gives an unscriptural answer, acknowledge that you heard him. See if another participant has a differing view. Ask, "What does someone else think about that?" The idea is to encourage participation. As people share from their heart, you will understand how to pray for them during the week. If you discern that further discussion with a participant is warranted, you may want to speak with that person privately after class.

Use eye contact and body language to encourage comments from quiet people and to control monopolizers. People will not want to return if one person talks too much. If necessary, speak to a monopolizer in private, enlisting his help in drawing out the quieter participants.

Above all, be sensitive to participants. Make them feel welcome and accepted for who they are. Listen to what they are saying and not saying. Ask God to help you see them as He sees them.

Some lessons include a time for participants to deepen their commitment to the Lord. The "Introduction" page that begins each series will alert you to those special lessons. Allow enough time in that lesson for interested participants to make that commitment.

Try to end each lesson on time. Participants will be more comfortable coming next time if you end on time.

Close With Prayer
Close the lesson with a short, simple prayer related to the lesson, e.g., in *Who Is Jesus*, Lesson 1, you might pray, "Jesus, help us value what is eternal more than what is not eternal. Help us desire a close relationship with you more than possessions or status. Amen."

Importance of Prayer

As facilitator, it is important that you pray for each participant between lessons, remembering that God is the One who draws participants into a deeper relationship with Him. Ask the Lord to reveal Himself to participants and to enable them to receive His love for them (Ephesians 1:17–19; 3:16–21). May He fill you with

His love for each participant and show you how to pray for each one.

Special Opportunity Lessons

During each of the three series, participants are offered the opportunity to accept Jesus Christ as their Lord and Savior. Lesson 6 in *Who Is Jesus?*, Lesson 4 in *Who Is God the Father?* and Lesson 5 in *Who Is the Holy Spirit?* all contain the wording you may use to lead interested participants in a prayer of salvation. Lesson 5 of *Who Is the Holy Spirit?* also provides participants the opportunity to be filled with the Holy Spirit.

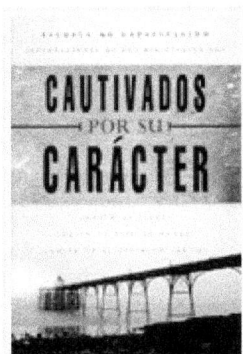

DO YOU KNOW A SPANISH SPEAKER WHO MIGHT LIKE TO KNOW GOD?

Captivated by Their Character is now available in Spanish as Cautivados por su Carácter. (Now also available in French). Go to contact@zoemin.org for details.

Others can come to know the three Persons of the Trinity and how they uniquely relate to us. Help them see how amazing Jesus is! Enable them to feel the love of God the Father for them. Watch the Holy Spirit transform their lives!

- Give your Spanish-speaking friends the gift of a personal relationship with the Lord.

- Send multiple copies of this valuable Bible Study series to a Spanish-speaking missionary you know.

- Use this book to reach out to Spanish-speaking neighbors.

- Recommend this book to a Spanish-speaking church in your city.

After completing these lessons on the Trinity, hopefully they will be captivated by Their character!

For a book description in Spanish, go to:
www.cautivados.com